STOP THE 21ST CENTURY HOLOCAUST

Ian Evans

AMERICAN TEENAGER

TABLE OF CONTENTS

CHAPTER 1

LIFE IS BEAUTIFUL

Life is beautiful, isn't it? I am a typical American high school kid. Like most kids, I go to school, do my homework, and attend school activities. I love to play games, watch movies, and spend time with my family and friends. And one of my favorite things to do is read. Reading enriches my soul. It helps me expand my imagination, understanding, and knowledge of this beautiful world where we all live together. I love to ask questions like: why are we here on Earth? how can we be happy? I want to understand the purpose of life for all humankind. I believe that life is a gift. As humans, it means we are here on

Earth only for a brief time. During our short visit here, every person should have the freedom to pursue happiness and try to live the best possible life.

Tragically, many people are not given the opportunity to be happy in this life. Even children can be caught up in the harsh realities of poverty, disease, and natural disasters. Perhaps the saddest form of despair is the one created by human beings. For example, during World War II (WWII, 1941 to 1945), some six million Jews were tortured and gassed to death by Nazi Germany and Nazi collaborators in what is now remembered as the Holocaust. Almost two thirds of all the Jews in Europe were killed during the Holocaust. No matter how many books I read about the Holocaust, I still have a hard time believing it actually happened.

We are all born as innocent babies. How can innocent children turn into such monsters? How can a group of humans do such horrible things to other innocent humans? How can adults murder children? The Holocaust lasted for four years. I still wonder how this atrocity was allowed to happen? Where were the reasonable people? If social media had been around back then, could global awareness have saved millions of lives? What if I were born back then-- what would I have done to help? After questioning myself many times, I came to the following realization: the Holocaust is an indescribable tragedy that should never be repeated on Earth again. After the death of six million innocent people, the world was awakened to the potential of large- scale evil, and reasonable people would now stand guard to ensure another Holocaust would never happen again! I thought to myself, what a privilege to be young in the 21st Century, full of hope, opportunities, freedom, and miracles! Life is beautiful!

However, in early 2018, while skimming through the news, a very disturbing title caught my attention, "21st Century Holocaust". I clicked the hyperlink and went on to read a story about how the Chinese government has put more than two million innocent Uyghur people into concentration camps. I read about how these Uyghur people are being tortured by the Chinese government. At first, I thought this news story must not be accurate. I did not want to think that it could be possible for a country as big as China to be engaged in the destruction of a whole minority people. I thought the world had already learned from the 20th Century

Holocaust, and I thought history was not going to repeat itself. But instead of walking away from this story, I decided to research more about these Uyghur people and try to find out the truth. At that moment, I actually could hear the voices and see the faces of the Jewish people who died during the last Holocaust, and they were crying out to me, "Do not let this happen again!"

Chinese police using armored vehicles on the streets of Urumqi, Xinjiang.

CHAPTER 2

IS THIS REALLY HAPPENING?

So I began to gather information from different news websites, magazines, newspapers. I watched testimony that was given to Congress. I watched Vice President Pence give a speech at The Hudson Institute. And as I painfully learned more, I found out that what the Chinese government has been doing to the Uyghur people is much worse than I had imagined. The Chinese government is secretly and quietly trying to eliminate the Uyghur people. The Chinese plan is not the same as the Nazi plan, but it is just as deadly!

Beginning in 2017, the Chinese government began executing its plan to eliminate the Uyghur people. Like the Nazis with their concentration camps, the Chinese government built 100 prisons in Xinjiang province. At the same time, the Chinese government demanded that all Uyghur people turn in their passports to the government. The Uyghur people would no longer be allowed to leave China without government permission. While the passports were being collected, the jails were being built. The Chinese government has now put more than two million Uyghur people into these concentration camps, and they keep arresting more Uyghur people every day. The Uyghur people who are now in these camps are not being released. If a family member asks when their spouse or child would be released, then that family member would be put into a camp. While many camps have been built in Xinjiang province, there are credible reports that tens of thousands of other Uyghur people are being put on trains and sent to Chinese prisons thousands of miles away. I can see the Jews on the trains, torn from their homes and trapped on a horrid train trip out of Germany to Aushwitz in Poland.

The information coming out of Xinjiang province is scary. In some Uyghur villages, there are reports that 60% of the population has disappeared into the concentration camps. Even more disturbing, there are also reports that the Chinese government has built many furnaces and are secretly exterminating and burning bodies. Unbelievably, there is a new holocaust happening right now in the 21st Century. This time, instead of Jews, it is the Uyghur Holocaust!

Sometimes, I wish I did not know what was going on, and I could go back to my normal life. I think to myself, if the leaders of the world are not doing anything to help the Uyghur people, what can an American kid do to stop the Chinese government? It is easy to think that there is nothing I can do to stop the Chinese government. Then suddenly that is when I had this important realization-- this is how regular Germans must have felt when the Nazis were forcibly relocating the Jews into ghettos. Today, Uyghur children are crying out for their parents. This is unacceptable. I will not look away while a corrupt government uses its state power to crush a helpless people. At home, I was taught to do the right thing. At school, I was taught to make the world better place. When I am old and look back at my own life, I will ask myself if I did enough. When I put myself in the shoes of the

Uyghur people, I feel their deep pain and despair. I can hear the Uyghur people asking, what did the world do to stop this appalling inhumane behavior? So far, I am sad to report that the world has not done much to stop the Chinese government. However, like a stone thrown into the middle of a pond, I believe one person can inspire others to inspire others. For I have an idea that together, we might be able to help save the Uyghur people. I have written this book because I believe in the power and goodness of the world's people. By pulling together, I think we can make miracles happen.

Uyghur woman crying for the release of her family members.

CHAPTER 3

WHO ARE THE UYGHUR?

From my study, I have discovered that the Uyghurs are a Turkic people who have lived in Central Asia along the Silk Road for more than two thousand years. In English, we pronounce Uyghur like "Wee-Gur" with the "Gur" sounding like "girl" without the "l" sound. Even in modern Turkey today, people say they are the descendants of the Uyghur people.

Traditionally, Uyghur people have lived in ancient oases towns along the Silk Road, such as Kashgar and Turfan. Before WWII, this area used to be called East Turkestan. After WWII, China claimed this land as part of the new People's Republic of China (PRC). The Communists renamed this area Xinjiang, with "Xin" meaning "new" and "Jiang" meaning "border". Now formally known as the Xinjiang Uyghur Autonomous Region (XUAR), it is the largest province in the PRC, one sixth of the entire country, more than two times bigger than Texas! Surprised? The Chinese government has done a great job in not letting the world know what's going on in Xinjiang.

The Uyghur people have a very rich and ancient culture full of dance, poetry, music, architecture, medicine and religion. If you go and visit an Uyghur village or spend time with Uyghur people, you will immediately feel that you are in a Turkish world. The smell of kebabs grilling around an open bazaar and middle eastern melodies playing from stores and homes is relaxing, mysterious and lovely. The mosques with their minarets are beautiful and different from our typical places of worship. The necklaces, jewelry and scarves remind one of Istanbul. Walking around a bazaar, you will see embroidered tablecloths, pillows, and carved knives. You are now in an older world, and the people there seem happy and have a great zest for life.

Uyghur Life and Culture

Spices in Kashgar Bazaar

Uyghur girls

Uyghur dance painting

Id Kah Mosque in Kashgar

Uyghur food

Zikh kebab

Homemade noodles

Samsa

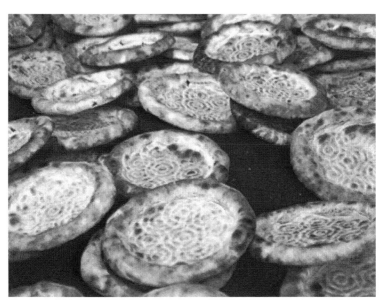

Nan Bread

More than 15 million Uyghur live in Xinjiang, and they make up the majority of the population. They live in cities and villages throughout the XUAR. For many years, the Uyghur were allowed to attend Uyghur schools where the students learned to read and write in Uyghur which uses the Arabic alphabet. For many years, the Uyghur people were allowed a bit of 'Autonomy'.

CHAPTER 4

WHY IS THE CHINESE GOVERNMENT PRACTICING ETHNIC CLEANSING?

Xi Jinping is the supreme ruler of China. In March 2018, the two-term limit that had been in place for Chinese leaders was removed. With no term limits, Xi Jinping is now the ruler for life. History is repeating itself, for a hundred and one years after China's last emperor Puyi finally abdicated the dragon throne, China has a new Emperor. Xi Jinping has done an outstanding job helping China become the most powerful country in the world! People used to think China was weak. Few people think that now. Under Xi, China continues to take steps to assert its power on the world stage. Perhaps Xi's most ambitious project is known as the "Belt and Road Initiative", the largest infrastructure program ever undertaken. Xi has created a plan to restructure global trade, and this plan includes a revitalized Silk Road with a new high-speed rail connecting China to Russia, Central Asia, Turkey and Europe.

For this new Silk Road transportation network to work, China feels it must have absolute control over Xinjiang province. The 15 million Uyghur people who live in Xinjiang are in the way of Chinese progress. So the Chinese government has decided that the Uyghurs do not need to have their own language, their own culture and their own religion. According to the Chinese, the Uyghur need to learn Mandarin, forget their religion, stop trying to be different, and learn to be good Chinese citizens. Any Uyghur person who disagrees, will be sent to a concentration camp.

Xinjiang province is mainly inhabited by Uyghur, though there are other minority ethnic groups, such as Kazakhs and Tajiks who also have their own unique and distinct cultural practices. The Chinese government is afraid that the Uyghur and other minority ethnic groups might rebel against China. So China fears losing this wealthy province. Xinjiang is very rich in natural resources. Xinjiang holds one-third of China's oil resources. Xinjiang also produces 60% of China's cotton. On top of all this, Xinjiang province makes up 1/6th of China's land area, but only 1% of the population. For the Chinese government, the problem question is simple: what is the most efficient way for the Han Chinese to gain complete control over the Xinjiang Uyghur Autonomous Region?

Their answer is chillingly simple-- the Chinese government must destroy the Uyghur people and gain absolute control over the Xinjiang Uyghur Autonomous Region.

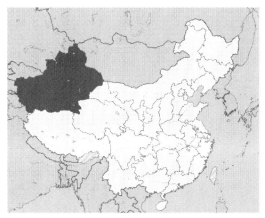

The XUAR region in red

Presence of the Chinese military in everyday life

Women begging the Chinese police not to take away or imprison their family members

CHAPTER 5

WHAT IS THE CHINESE GOVERNMENT DOING TO THE UYGHUR?

In August 2016, Xi Jinping ordered the Communist Party Secretary of Tibet to be transferred to Xinjiang province. This party secretary, Chen Quanguo, did a smashing job handling Tibet, and so now he will continue his inhumane work by smashing the Uyghur. Xi Jinping told Chen Quanguo to gain absolute control over Xinjiang province. So he has license to do whatever it takes to turn the Uyghur into Chinese.

After spending many years enforcing heavy-handed policies over the three million people in Tibet, Chen arrived in Xinjiang ready to expand his practices over the fifteen million Uyghur. Here is a brief breakdown of how the Chinese government, under Emperor Xi Jinping and Xinjiang Party Secretary Chen Quanguo, plan on reducing and destroying the Uyghur people:

The Chinese Plan to Destroy the Uyghurs

1. Take away all Uyghur passports and trap them in Xinjiang.

2. Build more than 100 concentration camps to torture Uyghur; tell the world these are vocational schools where they are teaching Uyghur important skills; if people say the Chinese government is lying, the government will say this is 'fake news'.

3. Arrest more than two million Uyghur.

4. Arrest all intelligent Uyghur professors, doctors, business people, artists, writers and even famous Uyghur athletes.

5. Put at least one person from each family in a concentration camp in order to control the whole family. If anyone asks where is my mom, dad, brother or sister, he or she will be sent to the concentration camp, too.

6. There are already reports of Uyghur women being raped in the concentration camps; if a woman complains about being raped, she will receive a lethal injection.

7. Put the Uyghur children of detained parents in closed schools where other Uyghur cannot visit or speak to them, basically camps for children.

8. Destroy Uyghur culture-- if anyone prays, does not take alcohol, does not smoke, or speaks the Uyghur language in public, they will be arrested. [in Uyghur culture there is a religious taboo against drinking alcohol and smoking]

9. Make Uyghur people renounce their religion.

10. Arrest those Uyghur who refuse to eat pork. [it is against the Uyghur religion to eat pork]

11. Inforce the Han Chinese to live in Uyghur homes.

12. Track their fingerprints and DNA.

13. Install surveillance cameras on every street, at every intersection, and use cutting edge facial recognition to track Uyghurs' every move.

14. Demand that Uyghur install GPS in their cars so the government can monitor driving 24/7.

15. Force Uyghur men and women to take sterilization pills.

16. If an Uyghur family in the US or Europe speaks up, kill their family back in Xinjiang.

17. Bribe other countries to forcibly deport Uyghur students back to China, secretly meaning to a concentration camp.

18. Secretly transfer around 500,000 Uyghur from the concentration camps in Xinjiang to Heilongjiang province and transfer 300,000 Uyghur to Gansu province. [Radio Free Asia reports Uyghur Detainees moved to prisons in at least five other provinces, including Inner Mongolia and Sichuan.] https://www.rfa.org/english/news/uyghur/detainees-02212019162142.html

19. Torture Uyghur emotionally, mentally, physically and kill them in the concentration camps.

20. Build furnaces in order to burn the bodies; learn more about this here: https://youtu.be/O9uQTjaUCQ8

21. Sell the organs of Uyghur adults and Uyghur children. http://eng.the-liberty.com/2018/7286/

22. Destroy mosques across Xinjiang, https://bitterwinter.org/a-case-study-in-destroying-faith/

Chinese Concentration Camp in Xinjiang Province, 2019.

New Chinese 'Reeducation Camp" in Xinjiang Province 2019.

CHAPTER 6

A UYGHUR WOMAN TESTIFIES TO THE U.S. CONGRESS

On November 29, 2018, Mihrigul Tursun, a young Uyghur mother, testified to the US Congressional Commission on China. The Commission is chaired by Senator Marco Rubio. The Senator states that this is the fourth such hearing on China's human rights violations with respect to the Uyghur people. This Uyghur woman's testimony to Congress touched me because she is not a journalist or mere observer. She is a mother who has survived a 21st Century Chinese concentration camp.

Mihrigul Tursun talks about the horrendous things she had to endure and witness in the concentration camps. By doing this, she is well aware of the huge risk she is taking by speaking out for she is endangering here family back home, and even her and her children's safety. In fact, later on in Mihrigul's testimony, she stated that she received a threatening call, telling her to take back all the things she said to Uyghur support groups in America.

Link to video of the full hearing:
https://www.youtube.com/watch?v=rrf8eW9xe7E

"Co-Chairman Rubio, Co-Chairman Smith, and members of the Commission, I would like to thank the United States government and the American people for saving my life and

bringing me to the United States of America, the land of the free.

Over the last three years, I was taken to Chinese government detention centers three times. I spent 10 months in the camps in total, and experienced physical and psychological torture at the hands of government officials.

Thank you for giving me the opportunity to testify about my personal experience in China's so-called "vocational schools" or "re-education centers."

My name is Mihrigul Tursun and I am 29 years old. I am of Uyghur ethnicity and I was born in Cherchen County in the Southern region of East Turkistan, the Uyghur people's homeland, officially called the Xinjiang Uyghur Autonomous Region. When I was 12 years old, I was taken to Guangzhou for middle school, under the Chinese government's program to move Uyghur children to inner China at a young age. This "Xinjiang Classrooms" policy takes thousands of Uyghur children away from their families, and immerses them in Han Chinese institutions, far from their native language and cultural environment. In effect, it forces the Uyghur to deny our cultural identity and religious beliefs, and to embrace the Chinese way of life. However, my experience in this state program actually made me more conscious of my ethnic identity. The constant discrimination and humiliation I experienced as a young Uyghur at a Chinese school in a Chinese city made me realize that I was different from the majority Han population.

I went on to study Economics at Guangzhou University and then worked for a private company that does business with Arab countries. I always dreamed of studying English abroad, and I finally had the opportunity to study at the British University in Egypt. On December 10, 2011, I left my homeland to study in Egypt, where I met my husband. In March 2015, I gave birth to healthy triplets, two boys and a girl, who are Egyptian citizens. I had difficulty taking care of my three babies, and on May 4, 2015, I left for China with my three two-month-old triplets to seek help from my parents. My troubles began the moment I set foot in China.

As soon as I came to the border control counter at the airport in Urumqi, I was taken to a separate room for hours of interrogation. My babies were taken away from me right at the airport. The authorities repeatedly asked me whom I met and talked to in Egypt. Then, they handcuffed me, put a dark sack over my head, and took me to a detention cener. I was not able to see or breastfeed my triplets.

After three months, the Chinese authorities told me that I had been "paroled" because my children were sick. They told me I could be with them until their health improved, but they warned me that I was still under investigation. They held onto my passport, identification cards, and cellphone.

I went directly to the hospital to see my children. My oldest son was in an emergency care facility and I could only see him through a glass window from far away, so I could not touch him to see if he was breathing. The next day, they gave me his dead body, saying he had been unable to breathe and they could not save him.

While burying my four-month old baby, I was tormented and filled with the guilt for not being able to save my son. My baby had been operated on while I was in prison. I was told that doctors had to insert a feeding tube into his neck. I did not understand why this procedure was needed as my baby had been breastfeeding without any issues before we left Egypt and should have been able to drink from a bottle.

My other two children developed health complications, and I spent the next few months seeking medical treatment for them, including an eye surgery for my daughter. They have suffered from health issues ever since.

I was unable to return to Egypt because all of my documents were confiscated by the authorities and I had been blacklisted. There was a black dot on my identity card, which beeped wherever I went: a hospital, pharmacy, and even a bus, so police would check my card and had to approve my every step.

In April 2017, I was living at home in Cherchen County when the police took me to a detention center for the second time to interrogate me about what I did in Egypt. The security department officials tortured me by interrogating me for about four days and nights without sleep. They shaved my head and closely examined me. They locked me up for around three months, and then released me to a mental hospital because I kept having seizures and losing consciousness. My father was later able to take me home to treat me and I gradually recovered.

In January 2018, I was detained for the third time for no reason. The authorities handcuffed me on my wrists and ankles, put a black sack over my head, and took me to a hospital. I was stripped naked and put under a big computerized machine. One female and two male officials examined my body while I was still naked and then dressed me in a blue prison uniform. It had the number 54 on it. A Chinese official reminded me that this outfit is usually worn by serious criminals who face capital punishment or life-time imprisonment and that "54" in Chinese also meant "I am dead."

I was very scared thinking this could be it, and I would die in this camp. I was interrogated for about three days and nights. During these interrogations, they asked the same questions: "Who do you know overseas? Who are you close to? Which organization do you work for?" I think, because I lived overseas and speak a few foreign languages, they tried to label me as a spy. My hands bled from their beatings. They also gave me drugs twice, and checked my mouth with their fingers to make sure I swallowed them. I felt less conscious and more lethargic, and lost my appetite after taking these drugs.

Then they took me to a cell, which was built underground with no windows. There was an iron gate and the door opened through a computerized lock system. There was a small hole in the ceiling for ventilation and we were never taken outside for fresh air. There was a toilet bowl in the corner out in the open without toilet paper. There were cameras on all four sides so the officials could see every corner of the room, including the toilet area. There was one light that was always on.

There were around 60 women kept in a 430 square feet cell so at nights, 10 to 15 women would stand up while the rest of us would sleep sideways so we could fit, and then we would rotate every 2 hours. There were people who had not taken a shower over a year.

That first night was very difficult. As I was crammed with other women on the floor with chains on my wrists and ankles also connected to a longer chain, I was thinking what I did wrong. Why am I here without any charge or explanation? What was my crime and why do I deserve such inhumane treatment? Why can't I use the bathroom in private and have toilet paper? Why can't I have water to take a shower or simply wash my face? Why don't I get enough bread to eat or water to drink?

We were awakened around 5am each morning with loud alarms. Then we had to fold the mere six blankets we shared. If the blankets were not folded neatly and looked symmetrical, the whole cell would be punished. They would take away the blankets so we would have to sleep on the cement floor.

Before we ate breakfast, which was water with very little rice, we had to sing songs hailing the Communist Chinese Party and repeat these lines in Chinese: "Long live Xi Jinping" and "Leniency for those who repent and punishment for those who resist."

We had 7 days to memorize the rules of the concentration camp and 14 days to memorize all the lines in a book that hails the Communist ideology. Those women whose voices were weak or could not sing the songs in Chinese, or remember the specific rules of the camp, were denied food or beaten up.

In theory, there were supposed to be three meals but sometimes there was no food all day and when there was food, it was mostly a steamed bun. I must note that the steamed bun we were eating got smaller and smaller as the number of people in the camp kept getting bigger and bigger. We were never given any fruit or vegetables.

They forced us to take some unknown pills and drink some kind of white liquid. The pill caused us to lose consciousness and reduced our cognition level. The white liquid stopped women's periods, though it caused extreme bleeding in some women and even caused death.

As if my daily life in the cell was not horrific enough, I was taken to a special room with an electric chair, known as the tiger chair. It was the interrogation room that had one light and one chair. There were belts and whips hanging on the wall. I was placed in a high chair that clicked to lock my arms and legs in place and tightened when they pressed a button. The authorities put a helmet-like thing on my head. Each time I was electrocuted, my whole body would shake violently and I could feel the pain in my veins. I thought I would rather die than go through this torture and begged them to kill me.

They would insult me with humiliating words and pressure me to admit my guilt. In fact, I had never been involved in any political activity when I was abroad. Then they would attack me psychologically and say "Your mom died the other day and your dad will serve lifetime in prison. Your son was in the hospital and he also died. Your daughter's eyes will remain crossed permanently, and she will be thrown into the streets because you cannot take care of them. Your family is torn apart."

This was very hard for a daughter and a mom to take. I felt a huge sense of guilt and worthlessness. I cried and begged them to kill me. I don't remember the rest. White foam came out of my mouth and I began losing consciousness. The last words I remember them saying was, "You being an Uyghur is a crime" and I fainted. When I first entered the cell, which was cell number 210, there were 40 other women, aged between 17 and 62. The cell was getting more and more crowded every day. When I left the cell after about three months, there were 68 women.

I knew most of the women in my cell. They were my neighbors, young daughters of my former teachers, and doctors, including a doctor, who had been educated in the UK and treated me in the past. They were mostly well-educated professionals such as teachers and doctors.

The most horrific days for me were when I witnessed the suffering and death of my cellmates. The nights were the busiest time in the camps; a lot of activities such as transferring people between cells or removing the dead bodies would happen at night. In the silence of the night, we would hear men from other cells groaning in agony. We could hear the beatings, the men screaming, and people being dragged down the hallways because the chains in their wrists and ankles would make terrible noise when they touched the floor. The thought that these men could be our fathers or brothers was unbearable.

Unfortunately, I witnessed nine deaths in my cell of 68 women in those three months alone. If my small cell, number 210, in a small county, experienced 9 deaths in 3 months, I cannot imagine how many deaths there must be now all over my country.

One victim was a 62-year old woman named Gulnisa. Her hands would tremble, she had red rashes all over her body, and she could not eat anything. She was really sick but the doctors in the camp determined that she was fine. The doctors at the camp were supposed to say the patients were fine because if they said the inmates were sick, they would be perceived as sympathetic or supportive of the patients. One night, Gulnisa was humiliated for not having memorize her lines in Chinese and she was crying when she went to sleep. She did not snore that night and her body was very cold when we tried to wake her up. She had died in her sleep.

There was another 23-year old woman named Patemhan. Her mom had died and her husband, father, and brother were all taken to the camps. Her crime was attending a wedding in 2014 that was held according to Islamic traditions, where people did not dance, sing, or drink alcohol at the wedding. She said all of the 400 people who attended that wedding were arrested and taken to the camps. When she was taken to the camp, she had left her two kids in the backyard. She had been in the camp for one year and three months and she agonized every day over the whereabouts of her kids. And besides that, she was bleeding for over a month and was denied any medical treatment. One night while she was standing with other women, she suddenly dropped to the floor and stopped breathing. Several people with masks came, dragged her by her feet, and took her away.

After all the torture and suffering I went through, I never thought I would come out of cell 210 alive. I still cannot believe it, but miracles do happen. Two hours before I was told I would be released, they gave me an unknown injection. I thought the shot would slowly kill me and began to count the minutes waiting for my death. I was surprised to be still alive when the authorities gave me a statement to read and sign. I read it and swore to it, and they filmed me doing so. The statement said: "I am a citizen of China and I love China. I will never do anything to harm China. China has raised me. The police never interrogated me or tortured me, or even detained me." The police warned me that I must return to China after taking my kids to Egypt and I must remember that my parents, siblings, and other relatives were at their mercy.

On April 5, 2018, after more than three months, I came out of that cell and was able to finally see my kids. I did not see my parents anywhere and was not allowed to ask about their whereabouts. I left my hometown three days later with my two children and stayed in Beijing for about 20 days because I was denied boarding the plane three times for alleged missing documents. On my fourth attempt, I was able to board the plane and landed in Cairo on April.28th. I was lost and in deep pain. I did not know what to do. My parents and siblings could be in those camps and the Chinese authorities could kill them if I do not return to China, but if I did return, I would go back to die in the camp and the truth of those camps would go back to that dark cell with me. And the Chinese government could still keep my parents and siblings in the camps or kill them.

I gathered my courage and decided to tell the world about China's hidden concentration camps so those people who tortured me and others would be punished for what they did and the voice of those innocent people in the camps would be heard.

Thanks to the help of many wonderful people, I was able to come to the United States. I cannot describe with words how I felt when I landed in Virginia on September 21, 2018. I was overwhelmed with the sheer joy of freedom and a deep sense of bewilderment that day. Did I already die in the camp and was now in heaven? Or was I really in this free and great country that I had always dreamed of coming to? It was too good to be true.

I currently live in the United States with my two kids. Even though I am no longer in a concentration camp, I have not been completely free from the traumatic experience and the Chinese government's harassment. My life is still haunted by sudden episodes of fear and anxiety as a reminder of the horrific days I went through in the camps.

My kids have physical and psychological health issues. They are scared when someone knocks on the door and afraid of being separated from me. I still have scars on my body from the constant beatings and pain in my wrists and ankles from the chains. I cannot hear in my right ear caused by heavy beatings. I am scared of the dark but also scared of too much light or noise. Police sirens give me anxiety and increase my heartbeat. Sometimes, I get shortness of breath, my whole body goes numb, and my heart hurts. I still have nightmares. Even though I was told I am safe here, I am still afraid at night that the Chinese police will knock on my door and take me away and kill me.

I also fear that Chinese government officials are still monitoring me. In fact several weeks ago, a group of Chinese men were following me outside and continued to follow me even after I got into a car.

The Chinese government must have also forced my brother to reach out to me. He left a voicemail on the cell phone I brought from China. My brother said: "How could you do this to your parents, to us? What kind of daughter are you? You should go to the Chinese Embassy right away and denounce

all the things you said about the Chinese
government in the interviews you gave to the
Radio Free Asia and tell them you love China.
Tell them you were pressured by the Uyghur
organizations in the US to lie about your
detention and torture in the camps, and take
back everything you said. Otherwise China
can get you wherever you hide."

I was terrified that the Chinese Government
could still threaten me from so far away. As I
am trying to start a new life in America, go to
school, work, and take care of my son and
daughter, I am still scared that the Chinese
Government will try to hurt me.
I will take this opportunity to kindly request
that the US Government take steps to provide
assurance for my safety. Exposing the real
nature of China's concentration camps puts
my life and my kids' lives in danger even in

the United States, so please do what is necessary to ensure that we remain safe in this country. Additionally, I was forced to swallow many unknown pills and given injections in the camp and I do not know what kind of drugs my kids were forced to take in while I was in the camp. I would really appreciate the opportunity to go through a thorough medical examination and treatment.

This is my story. But I am only one of the millions of Uyghurs and other ethnic groups targeted for punishment or death in concentration camps. I am blessed to have miraculously escaped the camps and I have the freedom to speak out on behalf of those being tortured in the concentration camps this very moment. .

The Chinese government made it clear that the cost of my speaking out would be the lives of my parents and siblings. I feel unbelievably guilty for that, and it is a form of ongoing mental torture I suffer every day. But I believe I also have a moral obligation to tell the truth to the world so that someone can take an action to stop this atrocity. My people look to the United States as the beacon of hope for the oppressed people around the world. While every other country in the world is turning a blind eye to this brutality to avoid falling from China's grace, I want to tell the truth to the government of the United States, the most powerful country in the world and the only country that has the courage and the ability to tell China to stop its ethnic cleansing of Uyghur people.

I hope that the United States will lead the world community to condemn China's gross violations of universally recognized human rights, and pressure China to close these concentration camps and release millions of innocent victims. The Chinese government's systematic abuse of Uyghurs and other minorities demonstrate that it thinks it is too powerful to be held accountable for its crime to eliminate the Uyghur as a people.

If the U.S. Congress passes the Uyghur Human Rights Policy Act of 2018, and imposes sanctions on the Chinese officials and entities responsible for carrying out the government's policy in these camps, China would realize that it cannot continue its crime against humanity and still remain as a member of the international community. Please help stateless Uyghur refugees around the world, who will certainly be taken to the camps if they return, seek refuge in this great country.

If any Member of Congress goes to China, please ask where my mother, father, and siblings are.
Thank you for your concern and attention."

After reading this testimony, I can't help but think of the other Holocaust. Some 75 years ago, there were Jews and other minorities suffering and dying in Nazi concentration camps. The good German people could not stop their own government. Other countries were not able to tell Hitler what to do. The invasion of Germany by Allied forces was the only way those concentrations camps and the madness was stopped.

CHAPTER 7

WHY IS NO ONE ABLE TO STOP CHINA'S HUMAN RIGHTS ABUSES?

From my research, it seems that there are at least four main reasons why it is difficult to stop the Chinese government from hurting the Uyghur people.

The first reason, economic power: the governments of other countries (including the United States) are afraid of the Chinese government's economic power. China is now the second largest economy in the world. Nearly everything around us is "made in China". For many countries, the idea of no longer buying inexpensive goods from China or not being able to sell goods and services to China is scary. In fact, the U.S. is $1.2 trillion dollars in debt to China, or 19 percent of the U.S. Treasury. Trade is a very big deal! Tragically, governments of the world, shamefully including the United States, are afraid of bringing up China's human rights abuses for fear of upsetting the Chinese government. This was sadly and shockingly evident in the recent trade talks of 2019 between the U.S. and China.

The second reason, investments. The Chinese government is either making low interest loans, investing in large infrastructure projects or purchasing government bonds in many countries around the world. The money coming from China is buying the silence of world leaders. For example, in 2017, Egypt deported more than 60 Uyghur students back to China, where they were imprisoned, tortured and at least two graduate students died in police custody. Now, China is funding a large new development project in Cairo. Simply put, China is bribing politicians around the world.

The third reason, propaganda: the Chinese Communist Party has successfully propagated a narrative in which they painted the Uyghur people as 'terrorists', so they are somehow doing the world a favor by killing Muslims. The Chinese Communist Party has locked up more than two million people whose one crime is their ethnicity! Actually, the true terrorists are Xi Jinping and Chen Quanguo who are responsible for severe human rights abuses and cultural genocide.

What is the difference between Xi Jinping and Hitler? Hitler killed millions of Jews secretly, and Xi Jinping has put more than two million Uyghur into secret concentration camps right now. The Chinese government has convinced itself that torturing a mother in an electric "tiger chair" is acceptable, that putting 60 innocent people in a 430 square foot cell for months and months without a shower, without any fruit or vegetables is acceptable. This is not acceptable!

The fourth reason, ignorance: not enough people know or perhaps care about China's human rights abuses. Not enough people see how dangerous China is. China has a long history of their government trampling human rights. During the Great Leap Forward (1958-1962), China's leader Mao Zedong brought about an unnecessary famine that killed 45 million Chinese people! The world did not or could not do anything thing to stop the madness. Besides famine, an estimated 2.5 million Chinese were tortured and executed during the Great Leap Forward. More unspeakable madness occurred during the Cultural Revolution (1966-1976). The world froze on June 4th, 1989 when the Chinese government ordered the Chinese People's 'Liberation' Army to liberate Tiananmen Square from the unarmed college students who were seeking democratic reforms. Since Tiananmen, the Chinese occupation of Tibet has resulted in the deaths of more than a million Tibetans. And the Chinese government even decreed that peace loving and spiritually minded practitioners of Fa Lun Gong were the enemy. Beginning in the late 90s, Fa Lun Gong practitioners were arrested by the tens of thousands. They were tortured, killed, and their bodies were used for organ harvesting. This makes me sick. In 2017 and 2018, reports came out of Xinjiang that Uyghur organs were being harvested, even the organs of Uyghur children. In fact, at the airport in Kashgar, Xinjiang, there is a special lane for diplomats to pass through quickly. However, this special lane also includes signs related to live organs; see the following photo:

The photograph below shows a priority lane sign marked "Special Passengers, Human Organ Exportation Lane," that was installed in Kashgar Airport located in Xinjing Uyghur Autonomous Region – Kashgar is one of the ancient cities of the Silk Road.

The Chinese government figures there will not be enough people who know or care about what they are doing to the Uyghur people. While many outsiders do not know much about the Uyghur, social media can be a fast and powerful tool to learn about these atrocities that were once so far away. Good leaders like Senator Marco Rubio and Congressman Chris Smith are willing to understand what is happening in Xinjiang and to take a stand against the Chinese government, although so far, this seems too difficult for politicians to carry out.

There are not enough people taking this issue seriously. Most people think this has nothing to do with their lives. The Chinese government is banking on the world being too lazy or too afraid to do anything to help the Uyghurs. By the time good people comprehend the fact that the Uyghur people are being torn to shreds by the Chinese government, it will be too late to save them. It would be perceived just like two-thirds of Europe's Jews: what is done is done. China might even blame one Chinese official and punish him to show the world they are sorry. That is the Chinese government's plan. So far, everything is going exactly as planned! To add insult to injury, the Chinese government has even succeeded in making large swathes of the world believe that they are the "good guys", and that they are bringing peace and stability to Xinjiang. They would say they are "helping" the Uyghur assimilate into China. Xi Jinping travels the world as the leader of the second largest economy on Earth, appearing so respectful and intelligent, so modern and civilized. Yet he is directly responsible for state sponsored ethnic cleansing on a scale not seen since Nazi Germany.

The Chinese government, with their army of censors and their surveillance state, are master manipulators, liars, torturers, murderers, and they seek to control the world. Because so many nations rely on China trade, or investments & loans from China, they will not stand up and call China out for human rights abuses. Therefore, the Chinese government remains highly confident about their ability to engage in long-term ethnic cleansing.

Throughout history, Chinese emperors could slaughter people like animals, and there would not be any immediate consequences. The citizens in China traditionally belonged to the emperor. Now, the citizens belong to the Chinese Communist Party, and its head, Xi Jinping. Chinese now follow Xi Jinping as they previously followed Chairman Mao, as the Nazis followed Hitler. To illustrate further, in the 1980s, 42 mass graves were discovered around the tomb of Qin Shi Huang, the great Chinese emperor who built the beautiful tombs full of terracotta warriors around 220 BC. The mass graves hold the bones of **700,000** craftsmen and laborers who dedicated nearly four decades to building the tomb they would later share with their Emperor.

Xi Jinping is now elevating the game of control by using artificial intelligence, GPS, facial recognition with good old-fashioned beatings and torture to accomplish control over roughly 20% of the world's population. In olden times, China was ruled by Emperors. Today, Xi Jinping has declared that China will exercise full control over the land, natural resources and people who inhabit the Xinjiang Uyghur Autonomous Region. During the last two years, more than two million Uyghur have disappeared, including women and children.

The sad news is that Xi's plan for control over the Uyghur and Xinjiang province is working. Not many people are willing to stand up. Even though this major human rights disaster has been brought to the attention of the United Nations, the United States Congress, and to the attention of many other countries around the world, the collective response from the world has been deafening silence!! This is the saddest fact...

Newspapers, magazines and websites from around the world have reported on the ongoing cultural genocide and mass incarceration of the Uyghurs. Nevertheless, the Chinese government continues its horrendous policies in Xinjiang. The Chinese government is still telling the world that they are helping to educate the Uyghur people in

what they have termed 'vocational' camps!
The mass incarceration and torture of the
Uyghur people continues.

Innocent people, such as the respected
Uyghur professor of economics, Ilham Tohti,
are rotting away in these concentration
camps. There are more than a million like him.
Where is China heading with these criminal
acts? Now, their claws are reaching out into
the world, including the United States. They
are spying and trying to exercise control even
over US citizens.

For example, if a US Professor writes or
speaks the truth, the Professor won't be
granted a travel visa. If an Uyghur American
speaks up, that Uyghur American's family
back in Xinjiang will be persecuted. By saying

nothing, by doing nothing, the world is telling the Chinese government that it can do whatever it pleases. There will be no consequences. By not standing up, we are giving the Chinese government more power, and we are giving them control. We are helping to make China's ultimate dream come true: to become the most powerful nation in the world. The question is: then what? Will the torture, killing, lies and bribes all suddenly stop? What can we do now to help the Uyghur and, above all, protect our world from the Chinese government's inhumanity?

CHAPTER 8

SAY STOP! WHAT YOU CAN DO TO HELP

As a high school student, I shudder when I see photos and hear stories about the tragedies of the world. In 2018, there were many other tragedies happening, and each of them broke my heart, such as the ethnic cleansing against the Rohingya, five million refugees displaced by the war in Syria, and 800,000 cases of cholera, the worst epidemic in recorded history, due to the war in Yemen.

In our classrooms, we learn about WWI and WWII, and we commemorate the innocent victims of these global conflicts. We are taught that "those who cannot remember the past are doomed to repeat it", yet humans seem unable to stop repeating the savage injustices that arise from greed and selfishness. In Washington D.C., millions visit the United States Holocaust Memorial Museum, dedicated to remembering the six million Jews who died in the last Holocaust. But right now, for the Uyghur of Xinjiang province, there is no freedom or human dignity, and millions of lives are being crushed and killed in horrific ways. Uyghur are dying in concentration camps; they are being tortured physically, spiritually and emotionally. This is a systematic, state-sponsored program of genocide, and the Chinese government is escalating this program on many fronts. Years later, are we going to build another Uyghur Holocaust Museum next to the Jewish one?

What action can we take now to stop the Chinese government from destroying the Uyghur people?

If I told you that by just spending a few minutes of your time, playing one less game or watching one less movie, you could change the world-- would you believe me? Imagine, if you see a child drowning in a swimming pool, just by reaching out your hand, you can literally save that child's life, right? We may think changing the world requires a great amount of money and effort. Yet sometimes, a very small action can bring hope to humankind and even save lives!

So here are a few simple things you can do to make a difference and change history. As a student myself, I know you have a very busy schedule. But some of my ideas below only require you to spend one minute! If you have more time, do more. If you have other ideas, share them. We need more heads to make miracles happen. When we come together and raise our voices, we can change the world. Let us bring light to those who are suffering in the darkness. Let us be heroes and bring about freedom. Let us stop history from repeating itself.

1. Use your social media voice for this good cause. Right now, simply post "STOP 21st Century Uyghur Holocaust" on your Instagram, Facebook, Twitter or Snapchat accounts. Ask your friends to share your message. If your message goes

viral, you will play a direct role in saving lives.

2. Raising awareness is great, but we also need to take action! So, send a letter to your US Congressional representatives and US Senators. Ask your friends in other states to contact their representatives. You can take an active role in waking up our leaders to pressure the Chinese government to STOP torturing and killing the Uyghur people. Do not wait for tomorrow. You can make a difference right now. There is a sample letter for you to use, after this chapter, at the end of this book.

3. After you have sent your letter, you can talk to fellow students, your

teachers, parents and friends about what is going on. Let them know the Uyghurs need their help. Send them the instructions and letter and ask them to contact their representatives, too.

4. Mark your calendars for Sundays at 12:00 noon, and no matter what your religion, ethnicity, political beliefs, post again, "STOP and Free the Uyghur!" By spending one or two minutes one day a week, you can raise your voice to help a people who are dying in Chinese concentration camps just because they were born Uyghur. Ask your friends to share your message or raise their own voices. Please do not underestimate your

power- 1,000,000 begins with the number 1. Be the one and be proud.

5. If you are a natural leader, you may want to organize a protest where you live. Talk to your friends, decide on a day and time, make signs, and stand on a busy street corner. Your signs can be simple, "Free Uyghur" and "Stop 21st C Holocaust". Your right to peaceful assembly is enshrined in the first Amendment of the US Constitution, a right that Chinese citizens do not enjoy.

6. Write to Google, Facebook, local newspapers, and your favorite websites, and ask them to inform people about the 21st Century Holocaust. Ask them to be a force for

good and to help change history. Ask them to place ads and banners stating, "Free the Uyghur People" or "Stop 21st Century Holocaust and Save the Uyghur". They may lose money in the short run, but in the long run, they will be the companies that stand for something more than money. But some do not seem to care: for example, Google has been working to develop a "censor friendly" search engine called "Dragonfly' tailored for China; and for instance, if you search for Orwell's political novel "Animal Farm", the information will be "0" -- this is truly terrifying censorship!

7. If your family likes to travel, ask to travel to Xinjiang. If the Chinese government does not let you go,

make a big deal out of it. Ask why?
Make some noise in the news.

8. If you are an Uyghur outside of China,
   ask your local government to help you
   locate any friends or family members
   who may have disappeared into a
   Chinese concentration camp. Do not
   give up hope! Good people care
   about you.

9. If you are a Chinese student or citizen,
   saying STOP to the Chinese
   government may be very dangerous
   for you, and you could end up in a
   concentration camp yourself.
   However, we know many of you are
   willing to help. For example, a very
   special Chinese student who was
   studying in Canada is the one who

located many Chinese concentration camps in Xinjiang province. These brave Chinese give the world great hope. They are the light to the world. Good Chinese people, please continue having the courage to stand up for justice, and while it is not easy, it will be worth it. We love you.

10. As we all know, celebrities have a great impact on society. Some celebrities have the passion and desire to do good in the world. Write to your favorite celebrities, ask them if they are willing to save lives simply by posting or saying, "STOP, and free the Uyghurs!" You might be surprised.

11. When you feel bad for the Uyghur who are literally dying at this moment,

please do not say, "Oh, I feel so bad for them, and I am glad this is not happening to my family" and move on to your daily routine. That is exactly what is happening now, and this is why the Chinese government is able to kill again and again until it is too late. Please ACT. Please give one minute of your time to think, pray, call others, say something, post on your platform, "STOP now! Unacceptable Chinese Persecution!" Please ACT now.

12. Educate yourself on this most important topic on the Internet. For example, you could watch Vice President Pence's speech at the Hudson Institute on October 4, 2018, where he details a major shift in US-

China policy and explains many of the crimes committed by the Chinese government; although unfortunately, no action has been taken by the US government, it's at least a small step in the right direction. https://www.c-span.org/video/?452478-1/vice-president-pence-intimidated-china

13. If you are an employee of any government in the world, do not bow to China's request to deport Uyghur back to China. Do not send an Uyghur refugee back to China. Do not send Uyghur students back to China. Please don't help the Chinese government torture and kill an entire race of people. Please do not partner with China in ethnic cleansing, no matter how much money they offer

you. Please say, "No", and please say "STOP!" You can stop China through your own act of courage. You will build a better country through principles, not through corrupt money obtained by looking the other way while China commits genocide.

In Conclusion

As a high school student, I am still full of hope and the belief that life here on Earth is meant to be beautiful. I believe in the power of humankind getting together to accomplish miracles. Together, we can change the world. Let us prove to China and the world that money cannot buy everything. Money cannot be used to purchase the silence of all humankind. Let us all cry out and yell, "STOP!" Countries, please have the courage to choose principles over convenience. Let us yell, "No, money will not keep us silent!" Let us yell, "No, money cannot be used to purchase human lives!" If you are a leader, inspire your audience by setting a real example for righteous governance. Be a great example by keeping your promises, and acting with integrity and honesty. Do not yield to the economic power of evil politics. We depend on you. To the youth, you are the future for this world. Let us create the world that we want to live in, so our children will look back to this time and be impressed by how we changed the world! We can save the world and change history. Why? Because we are fearless. We have morals. We care about right and wrong. We care about the truth. We have pure love in our hearts. We are not polluted by money or politics. We believe life is beautiful.

Even though we don't know any Uyghur people, we know that they are human beings, just like us. We know they have families, friends and loved ones, just like us. We know they breathe in air, just like us. We know they have the right to pursue joy and happiness, just like us. Therefore, we can say they are our brothers and sisters. All lives matter: Black lives matter, and Uyghur lives matter, too. Like Congressman Yoho said during a Congressional hearing on China's Repression and Internment of Uyghur, *"As we see over and over again, China leads by lies, deceit and coercion…They say one thing, and do something else. They speak deception, while they do underhanded things…I can't think of anything more Orwellian on the planet than what China is doing."* and again, *"I think what we are seeing here is a repeat of what we have seen too many times in history. And shame on us, shame on the free world to turn a blind eye and not stand up to this --- and how do you stand up to it? Can one nation stand up to it? Or does it take the whole world?"* Let us say, "STOP!"

Believe it or not, sometimes saving someone can result from a simple small action. We have the power to stop this 21st Century Holocaust. We need your help. Each one of you can help. We simply need to stand up and say, "Stop!" Not just for the Uyghur, but to save all humankind. Hitler did not decide to stop the Holocaust. People had to take action against Hitler. The world stood up in South Africa and said, "End Apartheid!" So just like that, I implore you! Citizens from all countries, employees from companies around the world, religious members, the young and the old --

all individuals— please, time is running out!! Let us remember our humanity! Let us speak out loudly and clearly to the Chinese government, "**STOP the 21st Century Holocaust!!!**"

Sample letter to the US Congress, I found on the internet:

Date:

The Honorable (full name)

United State Senate

Washington, DC 20510

Dear Senator:

As a constituent, I would like to bring to your attention the plight of millions of Uyghur people who face some of the world's most abusive human-rights violations and risk total annihilation at the hands of the Chinese Communist Government. An economically and militarily growing Chinese dictatorship is the greatest threat to the US national security, global leadership, and American values of freedom, democracy, and human rights that make this nation the beacon of hope for the oppressed around the world. Its president for life, Xi Jinping's grand design to project China's influence in Asia and Eurasia and displace US global influence, is the Belt and Road Initiative (BRI, also known as One Belt One Road). It has given Beijing a renewed motive to step up its crackdown in East Turkistan, officially known as the Xinjiang Uighur Autonomous Region (XUAR), and impose total control over millions of Uyghurs through an intense campaign of coercive social and political re-engineering.

Since 2017, the Chinese Communist Government has accelerated its "Strike Hard" campaign against Uyghurs in East Turkistan, BRI's core hub and gateway to Eurasia, with the ultimate goal of ethnic cleansing of Uyghurs. It has been detaining more than two million Uyghurs in secret "re-education camps,"

concentration camps where innocent Uyghurs are held without due process, brainwashed with Communist ideology, and tortured. The Chinese Government has turned the entire region into a 21st century police state through: ubiquitous checkpoints and high technology surveillance systems that monitor every aspect of Uyghurs' personal lives, coercive placement of Han Chinese in Uyghur homes, and compulsory interracial marriage. It has also been harassing Uyghurs living in the US and other Western countries to control their freedom to speak out against Chinese policies *by threatening retaliation against family members back home and it has cut off communication with the region.*

Please do whatever you can to stop the Chinese Communist Government from annihilating the Uyghur minority and to prevent another genocide that would stain 21st century world history. The US Congress should sanction, under the authority of the Global Magnitsky Act, the XUAR Communist Party Secretary Chen Quan guo and other officials and Chinese entities involved in designing and implementing these polices for their violations of international human-rights standards. Please support the efforts of Senator Rubio and Representative Smith, co-chairs of the Congressional-Executive Commission on China, and any future Congressional resolution to exert pressure on the Chinese government to cease its policy of illegal and arbitrary detention of Uyghurs, close those re-education camps, and allow an international investigation into its illegal arrest and torture of Uyghurs in these camps. The Chinese Communist government must not get away with its inhumane policy of forced assimilation and ethnic cleansing of the Uyghur people. China's model of surveillance is already inspiring other autocracies around the world and Uyghurs' tragedy today could become other nations' tragedy tomorrow when the Chinese dictatorship gains the upper hand over the free world.

Sincerely,

BIBLIOGRAPHY

Bugra, Otkur. "Understanding Uyghur Culture and Cuisine." Uyghur Academy. Last modified November 5, 2017. Accessed November 6, 2018. http://akademiye.org/en/?p=604.

China, Congressional-Executive Commission, director. YouTube. YouTube, YouTube, 29 Nov. 2018, www.youtube.com/watch?v=1WOem1tgDMc&feature=youtu.be.

Gulnaz, Uighur. "I'm a Uyghur Muslim who fled China's brutal crackdown - it's time the world showed us some support." Last modified Sept. 12, 2018. Accessed Oct. 25, 2018. https://www.independent.co.uk/voices/china-uyghur-muslim-rules-laws-treatment-chinese-human-rights-religion-a8534161.html.

Hollingsworth, Julia. "UN Boss Raises Xinjiang Uyghurs during His Trip to China." *CNN*, Cable News Network, 30 Apr. 2019, www.cnn.com/2019/04/29/asia/xinjiang-china-un-intl/index.html.

Karadsheh, Jomana, and Isil Sariyuce. "China's Persecuted Uyghurs Live 'Freely' in Turkey." CNN, Cable News Network, 12 May 2019, www.cnn.com/2019/05/12/middleeast/turkey-uyghur-community-intl/index.html.

Lichtenstein, Allisen. "XInjiang: The Free Expression Catastrophe You Probably Haven't Heard of." PEN

America. Last modified August 17, 2018. Accessed September 6, 2018. https://pen.org/xinjiang-free-expression-catastrophe/

Mailonline, Kelsey Cheng For. "China's Muslim Internment Camps Run like 'Concentration Camps', 'Turn Uighurs into Forced Labour'." Daily Mail Online, Associated Newspapers, 17 Dec. 2018,www.dailymail.co.uk/news/article-6504921/Chinas-Muslim-internment-camps-run-like-concentration-camps-turn-Uighurs-forced-labour.html.

"Representatives Sherman and Yoho Introduce Legislation to Stand Up for Human Rights in Xinjiang, China." Congressman Brad Sherman, 21 Dec. 2018. https://sherman.house.gov/media-center/press-releases/representatives-sherman-and-yoho-introduce-legislation-to-stand-up-for

Republicans, House Foreign Affairs Committee, director. "China's Repression and Resentment of Uyghurs." YouTube, YouTube, 26 Sept. 2018, Ross, Eleanor. "What's the History behind China's Current Obsession with Xinjiang?" Newsweek. Last modified March 10, 2017. Accessed September 10, 2018. https://www.newsweek.com/protest-xinjiang-china-muslim-central-asia-terrorism-559161. www.youtube.com/watch?v=O9uQTjaUCQ8&feature=youtu.be.

Ross, Eleanor. "What's the History Behind China's Current Obsession with Xinjiang?" Newsweek. Last modified March 10, 2017. Accessed September 10, 2018. https://www.newsweek.com/protest-xinjiang-china-muslim-central-asia-terrorism-559161.

Sales, Nathan, and Sam Brownback. "China's Attack on Uighurs Isn't Counterterrorism. It's Ugly Repression." The Washington Post, WP Company, 22 May 2019, www.washingtonpost.com/opinions/chinas-attack-on-uighurs-isnt-counterterrorism-its-ugly-repression/2019/05/22/7bfb1d60-7ccb-11e9-a5b3-34f3edf1351e_story.html?noredirect=on&utm_term=.fb53ab62261f.

Schrank, Aaron. "In LA, Muslims from China Watch and Worry as Homeland Crackdown Escalates." LAist, https://laist.com/2018/09/26/uighur_expats_call_for_action_on_human_rights_abuses_in_china.php

Senator Marco Rubio, director. Xinjiang's Human Rights Crisis. YouTube, YouTube, 26 July 2018, www.youtube.com/watch?v=WCjl0vRJMKs.

Staff, RFA. "US Lawmakers Unveil Bill Calling for Release of Uyghurs from China's Detention Camps." Radio Free Asia, Radio Free Asia, 14 Nov. 2018, www.rfa.org/english/news/uyghur/lawmakers-11142018152204.html.

Watson, Ivan, and Ben Westcott. "'Cultural Genocide': How China Is Tearing Uyghur Families Apart in Xinjiang." CNN, Cable News Network, 15 Nov. 2018, www.cnn.com/2018/11/14/asia/uyghur-china-xinjiang-interview-intl/index.html.

自由亚洲电台 , director. YouTube. YouTube, YouTube, 6 Nov. 2018, www.youtube.com/watch?v=HrZCGDliE8w&feature=youtu.be.

郭凯 , director. Human Rights Report Approved by UN Review - World - Chinadaily.com.cn. Human Rights Report Approved by UN Review - World - Chinadaily.com.cn, www.chinadaily.com.cn/a/201811/12/WS5be8b47ca310eff303287ea0.html.

Printed in Great Britain
by Amazon